Bound by the Sea

Bound by the Sea / *A Summer Diary*

Text and Photographs by Jean G. Howard

THE TIDAL PRESS

1986

Thanks go to Cynthia Williamson for her help in all aspects of printing the photographs from the author's negatives.

First Edition

ISBN 0-930954-25-4 HB

ISBN 0-930954-26-2 SB

LCC 86-50255

The Tidal Press, P.O. Box 150, Portsmouth, NH 03801
Catalogue available upon request

For Hilda

PREFACE

My name is Sandy Seymour. This is my school project for the summer—a diary. I'm told if I can impress my new English teacher, I can pass directly into Creative Writing. I've just finished Junior High and I hate grammar and spelling. This year I barely passed English—my spelling's lousy and grammar, to me, is worse than a foreign language. In a diary you don't have to know the difference between an adjective and an adverb, you just use them, and Father can help me with the spelling. Miss Speaks gave me nothing but Cs and even a C-. She won't listen to any of my ideas, and she won't even read my poems because they're not assigned. "Trying to get ahead of yourself, Miss Careless Commas," she'd say. "Tools, you have to learn the tools first." I don't see why tools don't go hand in hand with the job; knowing that you use a hammer to drive a nail doesn't teach you how to do it. But I learned to keep my mouth shut if I didn't want a D, and I tried to memorize the names of the tools and their uses. Memory has never been something I'm long on!

I've thought of a way to deal with the diary—Father gave me a camera for the summer and lots of black and white film (he says you have to start with black and white if you really want to understand the tools of photography!). He also gave me four books, one by Ansel Adams. I really dig his pictures, they're so dark and mysterious. The others are all about f-stops, speed and depth of field, and right now they don't make much sense, but Father says I'll begin to understand when I start using the camera.

Anyhow, my idea is to take lots of pictures and sprinkle them throughout the text. That way I won't have so many pages to write. Maybe my new English teacher will like what I do, maybe she'll see that I've got a few good ideas, so that's what I plan and that's what I hope.

June 1st, 1965

    It's summer again, or nearly. We left early because of my father's sabbatical. Why school let me go before the end, I don't know, but I didn't ask. We arrived today.

We've talked about it all winter, about going to Outercliff Island, the island where we've never been before. Mother says I'll like it! The drive up was hot and humid—I sweat all the way. We just made the afternoon mailboat, 4:00 o'clock, and everyone watched while we lugged our stuff aboard. I was embarrassed we had so much.

As I settled onto a hard slatted bench, and the boat's motor roared and shook its way out of the harbor, I realized I could see nothing. We moved blindly through yards of mist. The boat rolled on an uncertain sea and my stomach rolled with it. I felt as though I were leaving the familiar world and going into a most unfamiliar one. It wasn't only my stomach which felt uneasy.

The blanket of fog thickened and thinned as we plunged through it, teasing my eyes with possibilities. Sometimes I was sure I saw an object rushing towards me, only to have it dissolve before my eyes, as we passed through it. It was an eerie ride, which, thank God, finally came to a breathtaking end. The sky lightened and the town-landing was there before us, bathed in sunlight. As I looked back I saw the mountains of the mainland climbing suddenly out of their quilted bed of white. The tops of the islands, which we must have passed, appeared, the pointed spruce lining up above the fog like the guns of toy soldiers in a makebelieve world. Perhaps this was the beginning of a makebelieve summer!

June 3rd, 1965

At breakfast, I asked Father if he thought I should write in my diary every day. "Not every day," he said, "but don't skip too many or you'll find it hard to get started, again." That's what I thought, too!

Take yesterday; there wasn't much to write about— unpacking and looking over the grounds. But there is the house, not much to describe, like many houses we saw along the narrow-boredom-inland-road on our way east. We passed through miles and miles of scrubby woods and saw endless gray clapboard or gray shingled houses with gray yards and gray trash everywhere. Mother said, "Poor souls," but Father disagreed. "Lazy souls, lazy minds, lazy morals—feckless!" and then the great debate began about "advantaged" and "disadvantaged." I'm inclined to agree with Father; you either have it or you don't.

I started to tell you about this house. I didn't mean to suggest that it's neglected, but it is gray shingle and as Father says, "No style; not simple Early, fancy Victorian, or unusual Modern." He's right, it's just a hodge-podge of ideas thrown together—dormers, entries, a back woodshed, a bow-window, back and front porch and a brick chimney. It's comfortable enough inside. Lots of "bright work," as they call it here, spar varnish on yellow pine, and hardwood floors, polished and polished to a

frightening shine. Mother says she'll never be able to live up to the floors. I think she's right.

I have a room to myself, upstairs, with a dormer, slanty ceilings, cupboards and drawers built in and a narrow closet where the hangers have to go sideways. It isn't a large house, but it's plenty big enough for the three of us and my dog, SHAG. I forgot to tell you about Shag— she's a fun-loving, wire-haired dachshund with a smile on her face, a wag in her tail and fly-away hair. She loves me and I love her. Wouldn't you know she'd find the only sandy spot on the beach on our first walk!

June 5th, 1965

We're settled; at least I am. Today was my first chance to take my camera and explore. In fact I walked far enough to lose my way. It's funny how easy it is to get lost. There are many trails—deer, I'm told—that don't lead much of anywhere, but twist and turn you until you've lost all sense of direction. For a few minutes I was frightened, but excited, too, but kind of disappointed when I came out on the dirt road which leads to our driveway. I thought I'd gone much further, but perhaps that's because I stopped for a while in an enchanted forest where the dense spruce changed to airy birch; but it wasn't the birch which caught my eye! A stem, buried deep in a mass of green shiny leaves and neat white blossoms (bunchberries, I believe), rose to a beautiful pink orchid, a ladyslipper. Lying down on the prickly ground, I twisted and turned so that I could see the flower from every angle and take pictures of each one.

Next morning I sent the film off on the mailboat and five days later, when the pictures returned from the drug store, I couldn't believe the results. They were awful. The ladyslipper was lost in a maze of this and that—nothing had won out. I had wanted my ladyslipper to shine, but she was just a blob amongst a tangle of ordinary stuff. Too delicate for my talents, but I'll use this one that

*blurred. It has a kind of strength of its own. Anyhow,
when I got home that day, I wrote my first poem of the
summer, while my memory was fresh.*

Elegant Lady

*Elegant lady!
What a surprise to find you here in dappled woods,
Soft pink, firm flesh, thin, straight stem,
You outshine all I see in sun or shaded nook;
Surpass, I think, most other
Plain, everyday dull plants, without a name I know.
I'll take your picture, now,
Oh, Ladyslipper.*

June 10th, 1965

When the first batch of pictures came back on the mailboat, I showed them to Father. He thought some of them were better than I did. When I showed them to Mother, she flipped through the bunch making her usual flip remarks—"nice, oops, what's that one? a bit blurred, isn't it? this one I like, but some of them are just too gray." I think she was more honest.

Later, at lunch, Mother asked, "Why are there no people in your pictures?"

Before I could think of anything to say, Father said, "What does it matter? Some famous photographers took nothing but people, but others, even more famous, took nothing but landscapes. Maybe Sandy's a landscape artist."

I giggled. "Some artist," I said.

June 11th, 1965

At noon Mother, Shag and I walked the beach to the post office. Mother waited while I snapped some pictures, but I could feel that she was impatient to get on. The post office is a small building, right at the shore end of the boat-business dock, and its large window looks out to the harbor. The entry, where you wait for the mail-window to open, is tiny. It was crowded, everyone busy talking and joking, but not so busy that they didn't notice me. There were middle-aged ladies in pretty cotton dresses and men in work clothes and boots, skin weathered—I particularly noticed the hands—they looked like well used tools.

Though no one said anything to me, a few women greeted Mother. "Pretty day, ain't it?"

The only kids were two pimply faced boys and a real fat girl. They were fooling around. I listened. The older boy poked the girl in the ribs with his elbow. "Don't you know nuthin to sing but HOME ON THE RANGE?" His friend repeated the remark.

She gave as good as she got. "Ayah, but Miss Jones asked fur it. Kant say as I evah see such homely Ma and Pa bey-aas!" She giggled.

I gathered it was to be graduation night in the one-room school house and the pièce de résistance was The

Three Bears. *I got tired of listening and tired of waiting so Shag and I went to sit on the beach. It was a gorgeous day with fantastic clouds. Just right for pictures. I took some at the meter setting and then I took some one stop up and one stop down—this is called bracketing in my book. I knew from my other pictures that the average the meter suggested was too average for me. Like Mother, I hated gray pictures. I wanted drama and there seemed to be plenty of it around.*

June 12th, 1965

We did go to graduation and we did listen to those kids slaughter The Three Bey-aas. *I couldn't understand most of it, because of the clipped drawl of the islanders, but it didn't really matter for we all know the story of* The Three Bears! *The best part of the evening was the goodies afterwards—homemade cake with mounds of frosting, crunchy hermits full of raisins and the best crust I've ever tasted on an apple pie. I could have eaten twice as much but Mother had her eye on me.*

Father didn't pay much attention to Mother's eye— middle-aged spread or not—one of the advantages in being an adult.

I did get talking with two girls, Gracie and Adelle. They wanted to know if I'd seen the Heath and when I told them I hadn't they said they'd take me the next day. I didn't admit that I didn't know what the Heath was— Father told me on the way home that it was a large peat bog, and that I'd better be careful because walking through one of those could be treacherous; some parts of the bog had no solid bottom. Mother perked up at the mention of danger but I reminded her that she wanted me to make friends.

Luckily bicycles came with the house, so early the next morning, riding one, I joined the girls in front of the school. We sped part way down to the end of the island. We didn't talk much; we didn't have to, the wind blowing against our faces and tangling our hair. When they turned into a vague track which passed between two large summer houses, I slowed down. Adelle paused, turned around and shouted, "Cumin?"

"Where?" I asked.

"To the bottom of Orchard Road," Grace answered.

"Are we allowed?" I asked.

Adelle laughed, "Ben goin fur years. Ain't no one here, anyhow."

They bicycled off on the rough track with me on their heels. To each side of us were overgrown apple trees, that looked rather like my hair when it needs to be combed. No one had taken care of the trees for years. The road had been sinking between two banks as we bicycled down until we nearly smacked into a wall of a thousand round stones high above our heads. I could hear the sea banging the beach on the other side of it. We dumped our bikes where we were and climbed the grassy slope to the right, away from the sea. Low, scrubby trees and brush greeted us at the top of the rise. Grace and Adelle hunted around until they found what looked like just another deer trail, but which they seemed to know. We followed the trail slowly, because it had not been used recently and it was overgrown with brambles and roots. Blackberries and tiny rose bushes were everywhere. Soon, we were slipping down hill and when the path leveled off, on each side were swampy patches filled with skunk cabbage and ferns. With these I was familiar, but we began to pass something I had never seen before, large bunches of white cotton balls growing at the end of thin sticks. As I had brought my camera, I stopped to take pictures. The girls watched for a few minutes, but soon began to tease and shove each other. "Let's go," I said, tucking my camera into its case, but planning to come back another day, alone.

A bit further along the girls pointed out some handsome, bronze, shiny leafed pitcher-plants and waited while I snapped a quick shot. They didn't ask about taking pictures but I asked about the plants. "Aren't they supposed to eat bugs?"

"Ayah."

"Ever seen one do it?"

"Ugh!" they both answered. "Cum on."

Finally we broke through the brush and the Heath opened out in front of us. What an eerie place. The peat swells in a billowing pattern, the pattern of waves moving towards shore—moving towards me. There was steam rising, the heat of the morning sun "burning off" the surface wet, and wisps of fog dangling over the low ground. I shuddered. Father was right, it looked dangerous. KEEP OFF it seemed to say.

"Cum on," Grace called as she jumped from hummock to hummock, somehow knowing where to step and where not to step. I didn't dare remain behind but I *didn't like following her either. My sneakers were soon wet through, and several times I had to make a sinking jump for the next knoll. At last we came to a small, solid grass hump with a stunted spruce growing on it. Grace beckoned to me to come to the far side where she and Adelle were kneeling, looking at something. I was surprised to find on the edge of our grassy island a gathering of tiny wild orchids. It was so unexpected, a pure, gossamer pink flower on a clean thin stem growing out of this steaming, oozing swamp. When I got home I looked the orchid up in our* Field Guide to Wild Flowers *and I'm almost sure they were Fairyslipper Orchids. I thought it strange that the beautiful and the ugly should sit side by side, but when I discussed it with Father he said that if you really knew the Heath you wouldn't find it ugly, that too often something that you're unfamiliar with is frightening and therefore seems ugly and is unjustly blamed for the problems of the world. Father has a knack of turning an ordinary discussion into something ponderous. Sometimes I wish he wouldn't.*

It wouldn't be so bad if my day's story ended here, but what happened next is the ugliest part of it all. Without warning, Adelle grabbed a handful of orchids and yanked them out of the moss. "Going to take 'em home

and show 'em to Ma," she said.

"But they don't come back if you pull them up," I cried.

"How do you know?" She yanked another bunch.

"When I read about Ladyslippers, and they're orchids, too, it said you shouldn't pull them up because they grow from a little bulb at their root, the bulbs multiply slowly, and don't seed themselves all over the place like daisies. They're precious!"

"Who cares," Grace said as she grabbed a bunch for herself. "There's lots more."

"Where?" I couldn't see any more. I was furious. "You're Murderers!" I shouted.

They giggled. "You're a kook," Adelle said. "There's plenty if you know where to look." She grabbed Grace by the hand and hopping and skipping the marsh, headed home.

As near as I could tell, we went back the way we came, the two island girls carrying on as though I didn't exist. They didn't address one bit of conversation to me. But this suited me fine, for as I followed I bent a branch here and there for a marker, so another day I could find my way back.

June 13th, 1965

It's raining, so I've plenty of time to catch up on my diary. I just finished June 12th. In fact I'm writing more than I planned, working over it some. I don't think a diary should be sweat over like a school composition, but boy it's hard to say something so it comes alive, isn't all tangled with stumbling, stupid words. If it had to be perfect, I'd soon give up, but it's fun to try. I think I see why Father wants to be a writer; it's like a daily crossword puzzle where you make up the answers.

This morning Mother and I baked cookies. Baking on a rainy day is a good time to drop little nuggets of ideas along with the raisins and nuts to see where they fall. With Mother they can fall into an angry, boiling, sticky brew of jam, or into a peaceful simmering soup— I'm never sure which one it will be! I told her something about the Heath, things that wouldn't scare her too much, and then I told her about the girls.

"Those two, Grace and Adelle, are cruel. They didn't give a damn about the orchids, not really, but it's funny, Adelle did want to bring some home to her Ma. I wonder, was it really a gift, or was it sort of a way of bragging!"

Mother always has an answer. "Sandy, must you distort things! Of course it was a gift for her mother. I'm sure it never occurred to either of the girls that they were de-stroying something, but once you pointed it out, they certainly didn't want to admit, that you, a stranger to the island, knew more than they did. Remember, they haven't had your advantages!"

"Damn, it's got nothing to do with advantages, it's built into them. I've seen one island kid be real mean to another. Perhaps it's in their genes or something, but sometimes there seems to be nothing but meanness in the air."

"Nonsense, tolerance, my dear, or you won't make any friends."

I doubted that I'd make friends, anyhow. Once I tried to get my class to give money to save the Bengal Tiger instead of to The Cancer Fund—they thought I was nuts. Doesn't do any good to hit your head against a locked door, but I hate locked doors. At school I've one good friend—that's enough.

June 15th, 1965

Yesterday, the day started in foggy, but by lunch time the fog had lifted and the sky was blue with fat white clouds. Every bit of haze had disappeared. Where the haze goes is one of those mysteries that the weathermen have never made clear. Clouds drift but haze does a disappearing act. While we were eating, Father suggested that it was a good afternoon for photography, and since that fit in with my plans, I agreed. Mother said something about not going places where one might get lost and maybe there should be limits, but Father said, "Lost! On Outercliff Island! It's not a backwoods wilderness."

Again, I agreed.

My bike took me quickly to Old Orchard Road and down its bumpy length to where I heard the sea. It was very noisy, noisier than I remembered. I was glad to get away from it, as I ran along the tramped down deer trail, my camera thumping against my side. It wasn't long before I came to the cotton balls and pitcher-plants. Sitting amongst them, I took pictures at every angle, with lots of different settings and speeds. Still, when the pictures came back from the drug store, they were disappointing. I wasn't much better at capturing the dazzling effect of these wild plants growing in large bunches, than I was at a good close-up, showing that each white powder puff

A fly escapes the swatter,
But he's not home free.
To be eaten by a pitcher-plant
Might be his destiny.

had a different face. Here is a pitcher-plant with a verse, and an enlargement of the cotton balls—another day, another story.

Pictures taken, my next plan was to find the Heath and perhaps the fairyslipper orchids. I hunted for the twigs I'd snapped to mark the trail, but I never realized before how many twigs are already snapped. I tried path after path, dodging under branches and pushing my way through brush, until finally I came upon a place which opened onto the Heath. It probably wasn't the same place I'd been with the girls, because I couldn't find anywhere I could walk safely on the peat. Perhaps the rain had made the bog wetter, but each time, after a careful step from one hummock to another, my sneakers began to sink into the cold slime. It was very nerve-racking. I couldn't see any solid hump with a spruce tree—the only spruce trees I could see were far into the bog, much farther than I remembered going before. The mosquitoes were fierce. Their nasty hum buzzed in my ears and they landed on me wherever there was a bare spot. I hadn't even worn socks to protect my ankles. I was already itching in a dozen places. I didn't stay long. I turned my back on the bog and the orchids and began the trek home, at least I thought I was going home.

Soon I found there were thousands of trails and most of them ran out to nothing, well, not nothing, but to brambles, bushes and branches which stopped me dead. I was getting scratched and hot and my watch said 5:30. Mother liked me to be home by then to help with dinner. Finally I stumbled into a wide cut-off area (a logging road, I learned later). I thought it might lead me back to the main road, but I didn't know whether to go left or right. My instinct was to keep going right, but I guess this time my instinct was wrong, because after what seemed like an hour but was only ten minutes by my watch, I came around to a familiar place, it looked like the place where I had started from. There was a huge rock coming out of moss with yellow and gray lichen growing on it. It had a special quality which I remembered. My heart was pounding. I'd hurried so, I was gasping for breath, and my hip was sore from my camera banging against it. I thought of shouting, but I wasn't sure I wanted anyone coming to my rescue—how Grace and Adelle would laugh at my getting lost. I was very tired and felt tears gushing behind my eyes.

I collapsed by the giant boulder and leaned my shoulders against its solid surface—a kind of Rock of Gibraltar. I laughed uneasily, but laughter wouldn't get me

home. Sitting there, wondering what to do next, I suddenly realized that I was hearing the sound of cars. They had to be running up and down some road—probably the main road. It couldn't be far away, but I soon found out that sound in the woods travels in mysterious ways. At one moment I was sure it was near me and to my left, and a little later it seemed very far and to my right. The only thing that was clear was the general direction, and that, I hoped, would keep me from heading to the back shore where no one lived. I wished I had a compass, but I didn't. I realized the sun was sinking behind me, peeping through some tall spruce. I tried to keep it there and I hoped I'd reach the road before it sank completely.

I trudged along in what I thought was the right direction. I had to abandon paths and instead climb over dead, spiny branches which caught my slacks, and over low bushes which scratched me. I stopped a lot to listen. I wasn't sure that I was gaining for often the sounds were muffled and distant. It was getting harder to see. Tears were stinging my eyes, when much to my surprise I heard the grinding of gears right in front of me. So near! I didn't know if I could get through the brush and bog ahead, but I had to try. My feet sunk into the peat and water crept half way up my calf. It was the worst I'd been through. As

I pulled with my hands one leg out after the other, each step popped from the suction of the peat and the deep clay. I was almost ready to give up, but as so often happens when you're about to give up, the struggle was finished—there, in front of me was gleaming black tar, a road! I peeked from behind a bush but thank God, no one was passing. I could even see the Old Orchard cut not far off. I groaned and considered running home without my bike, but that would surely bring down the wrath of God and the wrath of my parents.

Pedalling hard along the main road, I watched a terrific sunset, an orange globe and sheets of lavender light disappearing behind the Western Mountains I raced this sunset to a tie finish, for dark descended as I rode in the driveway. I wished I could sneak up to my room, but no way. I listened at the door. I could hear Mother and Father arguing and the scraping sounds of knives on plates. I threw the door open and stomped over to the rocker where I collapsed, mud, bloody scratches and all. I won't go into what happened next—anger often hides love, I'd learned that much, but I was grounded for a week and had to promise that from then on if I was alone I would explore only well used paths or roads—no deer trails. It was a promise I intended to keep.

June 16th to 23rd, 1965

This week at home hasn't been so bad. I've had a lot to think about, and I got all that writing done about my day in the Heath. I wonder if anyone besides my teacher will be interested? Someday, someone else might read my diary. Are all diaries written with that secret half-hope? I wouldn't be surprised.

Nobody says a diary can't have poetry in it—well, maybe not real poetry but something like it. Father says poetry doesn't have to have rhyme and a repeated beat like poetry from the past, but, he says, and this is a direct quote, "The words must excite the imagination, must startle the mind with their apt originality, must move those who read them, but the reader must never lose sight of the subject. Clarity above all else. . . ." I would like to be able to do that in a poem.

I've plenty of poetic ideas, at least I think they are, and there are plenty of poetic things to look at around the house: the fields with wild flowers, the family graveyard just down the path, the beach, the sea—need I go on! Luckily Mother said I could go to our nearby beach if I'd take Shag. Why would I mind taking Shag, the love of my life! I don't dare take her bicycling because some people drive like crazy on this island. I think I'll start with the field and leave the beach till later; it's so pretty now filled with yellow, orange and red paintbrushes. They make a lovely pattern, with rivulets of colors running here and there, but how to show that in black and white! I'll try. I have learnt that it's no use taking pictures in the middle of the day when it's too bright—everything flattens out. It'll have to be early in the morning for paintbrushes close their flowers in mid-afternoon.

The grass grows in wild bunches after the rain.

The Indian Paintbrush spreads its colors for the bees.

There is an abundance.

The season is short but there is a season.

Will there always be an abundance?

Will there always be a season?

The day is past and gone,
The evening shades appear,
Oh may we all remember well,
The night of death draws near.

This is a family graveyard. There are many such grave-yards on the island.

The oldest stone, Capt. Thos. Manchester, has an ancient engraved verse, hardly readable. It looks at life and death in a way we seem to have forgotten.

The newest stone is sweet and plain: MOTHER and then her name.

The 15 graves tell the story of a Maine island, this island, from its earliest days to the happenings of today. Those lost at sea, those who died young from some fatal disease, he who gave his life for his country, a three-month-old child, a son who died the day he was born, a young wife and the old who have, GONE HOME, they are all here. Perhaps someday I can discover some of this story.

GILMAN J.

Son of Jonathan R. &
Irene Stanley
Drowned in the
Straits of Belleisle
June 18, 1861

Æ 16ys, 8m, 28ds

Break not the turf for my dear friend,
Nor part the dewy sod,
My body rests beneath the surf,
My spirit with its God.

MARGARET S.

wife
of
Samuel S. Fernald
Died
Aug. 30, 1867

Æ 27ys., 2m, 22d.

One we love has left our number,
For the dark and silent tomb.
Closed her eyes in deathless slumber,
Faded in her early bloom.

In Respect

There's a graveyard in my wood,
Where families gather—friend or foe,
There's parents there, and children, good,
The final resting place below.

A comfort for those here and now,
Before the world they disavow.

Slender Blue-Flag

An open marsh, an army of blue-flag;
A peaceful army, a joy to the eye.
A blue uniform with green sword at its side,
As far as the eye can see—standing tall.

Oh, slender blue-flag, your beauty reassures.
Oh, that all armies could only want your perfection.

Garter Snake

He is a giant amongst the grasses.
He spat.
He hissed.
I am his giant.

Waves

The pebble beach gathers the many waves.
They creep playfully up and up,
Polishing each stone on the flood.
On the wane, they release
The cleansing waters in lively streamlets,
Back into the sea.

How perfect this continuous cycle of moon and tide—
Man can not change it.
Let us pray that he never can.

June 24th and 25th, 1965

The clear, sunny week ended in fog, the kind of gray fog which drifts in and out and makes one's head swell with weariness. Atmospheric pressure, I'm told, but knowing why doesn't help—I still feel dumpy and depressed. Shag and I walked to the beach as we had most other days, but we had no energy. I sat in a sandy patch, running the sand through my fingers, like a slow hourglass which repeats and repeats its task, and Shag floated into the haze. It was as though the mist turned me into a mummy.

From somewhere I heard voices. At first they were muffled, then clear as a bell, and then muffled again. They could have been near or they could have been far, there was no way to tell. I liked the feeling of being invisible, of being able to eavesdrop without being seen. Even boats were a mystery. I could hear their engines, but at best their hulls were a dark blur behind a curtain. To me that was a friendly curtain, and I was sitting on the stage, a stage where I never needed to reveal myself, a stage where there were many possibilities. I could fill that stage with dreams which never had to be tested. Perhaps dreams, the kind one makes up for oneself, are the desserts of life which never should be tasted. We need dreams, but what Christmas was ever as good as you expected!

Today is the second dark day and since I could not summon up a dream, I came home to write. I find more and more I like working with words—words and ideas— what a challenge, it's so hard to get the words to equal the ideas! I suppose these ideas are just another kind of dream, so they're not easy to explain in words. After I'd worked all morning, my head was as fogged as the day, so lunch and dishes done, Shag and I went back to the shore. She was full of energy, dashing hither and thither. Even I felt a lifting of the spirits. Barefoot, I splashed along the edge of the tide, picking up pieces of sanded glass and strange rocks. Suddenly I felt a wind. The fog evaporated but there were still dark clouds hanging high over head. I thought there would be a storm but it never came. In the evening there was an awesome and marvelous sunset. After dinner, I ran to the beach and caught with my camera the last flash of light.

July 1st, 1965

Every day there are more and more strange faces along the road. Mother keeps telling us about nice Mrs. so-and-so whom she met at the post office—most of these ladies have been summering here for years. Then, today, without asking me, she promised a Mrs. Motley that I'd crew for her daughter, Nancy, in the afternoon's boat race. I know nothing about sailing! Mother said I'd learn. How wrong she was.

Nancy and her friend, Susan, were waiting for me at the dock. "You're Sandy, I suppose. Jump into the punt—we're already late."

"Yes," I answered. I climbed in, rocking the punt ferociously. I sat nervously wishing I could chitter-chatter the way chick-a-dees chitter at our feeder every morning, but I don't have any chit. Nancy and Susan did! Father's told me not to worry, small talk isn't as important as what you do with your talents. Mother doesn't agree. She says success, even satisfaction, could depend on both ability and sociability. She could be right.

I was supposed to handle the spinnaker. I'd never heard of one before but they were awfully pretty when they were all up. There wasn't much wind and a big swell. I got sea sick—and then, when I was told to bring in the spinnaker, I dropped it in the water. That was the end of my crewing career; not only did they not invite me again, they didn't speak to me all the way home.

July 2nd, 1965

Chores done, I begged Mother to let me go to the far rocks where I could take pictures of the open ocean, where I'd been told there was no land in sight. Mother agreed, if I stuck to the trail above the rocks, for she'd heard there was a safe trail along the north and eastern shore. I was to take no risks. I promised.

I bicycled to the path, and then after five minutes of walking through a gloomy canopy of thick spruce, I came out to blinding light. Once my eyes adjusted, what I saw was fantastic. Miles of glistening empty ocean, and thousands of pink boulders that had been tossed onto the shore by some playful giant, or so it seemed.

I looked and looked, gulping great gouts of cleanliness. The sea and the rocks had such a scrubbed and polished air and the air itself was washed by the sun, sweetened by the breeze, pure and clean in the best sense of those words. Everything around me was so alive, it had none of that death-like look of my maiden/uncle's house, where everything is clean, where there isn't a speck of

dust and nothing is ever out of place. I hastily got my camera ready and began snapping pictures, but as I peered through the view-finder what I saw was not what I felt. How to catch that feeling! How to make the picture come alive. I over exposed and under exposed and lay on my back and twisted to my side. My eyes saw wondrous things but would the camera? I was really lost in the world of rocks and sky, darks and lights, when I heard a voice, a deep male voice, say, "What make of camera do you have?"

Frantically, I wiggled my way out of my bed of rocks. "Canon," I answered, getting to my feet.

"Sorry," the voice came from a young man with a camera and tripod on his shoulder. "Didn't mean to startle you. Did I ruin your shot? Marvelous boulders, aren't they?"

"Yah, uh, they are." Then I asked a dumb question. "You take pictures, too?"

"Kind of looks that way, doesn't it!" He limped nearer to where I could see him better. "You live on Outercliff Island?" he asked.

While I was explaining my presence on the island, I was making a quick survey—he was tall and slim, blonde and attractive but there was something oddly awkward about his body. I soon found out that I was trespassing on his parents' land, the Stuarts. He assured me that it was okay for they kept the trail along the rocks opened for the use of the general public. What they didn't like was to have people snooping around their house, which was somewhere above us on a high hill—"Tremendous view," he said. He told me he was making his way down to where the gray rocks started—had I seen the seam which divides the pink granite from the gray stone? We walked together to the place he was telling me about, something to do with the ice-age, but to me it was a miracle. Except for a few non-conformers who'd been tossed from their proper place by winter storms, every rock on one side of the line was pink and white and every rock on the other was black or gray, with an occasional warm rust spot.

"It's like age meeting youth," I said to Bob, for that was his name, "round and rolling pink-faced youth meets stiff and rigid gray-lined age."

He laughed. "I see you prefer fantasy to fact. What about, 'architectural design wins over chaotic inspiration'?"

I laughed, too. "I'm not sure about the 'wins,' maybe there's room for both."

For a while, we stood and admired nature's design, but soon I said I'd better get back, obviously he had photos he wanted to take. After I was well out of sight, I found a comfortable niche which fitted my fanny and where I could lean against a rock wall. The tide was coming in. I watched a long time the endless movement of the swell.

I Wonder Why

Oh, most lonely wave, where do you come from?
From what ocean depth has your shape been born?
What force rolls you on and on, repeats you as one?
I see the same face over and over,
Or nearly—somehow, brothers and sisters
You surely must be; chasing each other,
Then losing yourselves on the rocks below.
If I come tomorrow, will you have gone? or perhaps
Not gone, but that day, not even started!

We all have to start somewhere, born from a kin-source;
But do we know why!
Oh, wave, do you care?
I do.

July 3rd, 1965

I want to keep Bob to myself. If I meet him again, will he even speak to me? And I can hear Mother, "Have you seen Bob; no; why?" and then there is this negative feeling I have. When I was the only serious photographer on Outercliff Island, I had a kind of freedom to try anything, but now that there's Bob with all his fancy equipment and knowhow, it's different. Silly of me, I know, but I can't help it. Jealous, I guess, competing again, like school—it's silly, silly, silly—I'm sure he doesn't think of me as competition, so why should I! We're scarcely part of the same world!

Well, believe it or not, tonight at dinner, Mother and Father were talking about the Stuarts, and before I could stop myself, I blurted out, "I met Bob on the rocks, yesterday."

"You did!" Mother said. "What's he like?"

"Okay," I said, "takes pictures, too."

"I suppose that's something he can *do," she remarked. "He had polio as a child, and his family were devastated. The only son, you know, and his father was a great football player at Harvard. Hardly speaks to the boy, they say."*

"Oh, that's why he limps," I said, but I thought, how strange that families expect their children to take after them, when so often they don't. Even if he hadn't had polio, he might not have liked sports, and the way Mother said, "I suppose he can *do that"! What does she know about photography's place in this Modern world! She's as bad as his parents—Doctors, Lawyers, Professors, there are other things to do with your life, in fact, most of the world does other things—but what was the use of saying anything.*

July 4th, 1965

Another cold, foggy day; Maine weather is sure changeable. One day is so hot and heavy that as you walk through the fields you're breathless—the air is dense with the dust of flowers and grass, happy for bees but not for me; then the next day can be so clear and crisp that it lifts you a mile high in expectation; and then days like today, they plunge you into a clammy decline. We dragged ourselves to the beach, Shag and I. She sat quietly beside me, giving an occasional discontented shiver, while I watched the gulls swooping and swirling in lazy patterns. I took some pictures. Here's what they were like—not much more exciting than my memories, though perhaps their blurred haziness gives you a feeling of flight. Gulls are the best fliers.

In the afternoon, Mother and I made a cake to take to the picnic. She doesn't make them often; she says Father and I can well do without cakes! I've always wondered if for a month I could have all the cake I wanted, I'd stop wanting it. I doubt it.

Tonight there's a Fourth of July picnic that ends with fireworks. The fishermen provide lobsters and clams; the women cake. I remember when I was little I could hardly wait for nine o'clock to come around, when it would be dark enough to start. Now, I don't even want to go. I'm sitting here praying the weather'll get worse and everything'll be cancelled. I hate group activities.

> *To sit on the beach all by yourself,*
> *When others are laughing around you,*
> *Is torture, you see, of the first degree,*
> *A hell here on earth—or maybe a freeze—*
> *I've been frozen before. You never quite thaw.*
> *SO—who needs it!*

The sun's coming out! The tide's low. I'm going musseling. Maybe I'll break a leg!

Mussels are clean but tough
To pull from their beds in the sea;
You scrape your knuckles and crack
Your nails, and all you've got is three.

July 5th, 1965

Well, you can't believe what happened last night! I'd gotten my lobster and a rock to bust the claws and I was sitting far away from the fire, up where rose bushes meet the pebbled beach, the dark scent of many flowers tickling my nose, when Bob's voice boomed out beside me, "Like picnics?"

"Not big ones," I said, "I prefer small picnics of about two."

He threw back his head with an awkward thrust and laughed. "I'm inclined to agree. What about fireworks?"

"Fireworks are unreal!" I answered, "but they're over too soon. If we could only pin them to the sky at the peak of their flowering . . ."

"I know what you mean. I'm going to try with my camera, with fast color film, but I'll need some help."

"Help. I'm a good helper but I don't know much. Do you think I'd do?"

"You'll do," he smiled and sat down to eat his lobster.

The tide was high, so when we were finished we were able to wash our hands in the sea. There's no way you can eat a lobster on the beach without getting sticky. Then we made our way to his car, where we picked up his camera and tripod. From past experience he knew in what di-rection the fireworks would be shot. We set up the tripod on a less busy part of the beach, and with a certain amount of difficulty he adjusted the camera. When the fireworks started, he wanted me to scrunch down where I could check the viewfinder. He said he would be unable to do that. Then, if I'd yell, "NOW" whenever there was a good shot in the finder, he'd snap the pictures with his button release. While we waited for things to start, he told me about his darkroom, he even invited me to come and he'd show me how to develop a film and he'd teach me to use his enlarger. I didn't hesitate to accept the invitation. I hadn't noticed it was dark, when I heard the first bang followed by a weak golden shower. The next one was better, but I was soon too busy to be much of a critic—to really see the fireworks that night, I'd have to wait for the darkroom and Bob's prints.

July 7th, 1965

Had a terrific time yesterday. Wow! does Bob have a neat darkroom. He has everything: an enlarger, pans, chemicals, red lights and running water. He showed me how to enlarge and crop one of his pictures in order to get a better effect. Next time I'm to bring a negative of my favorite shot, and we're going to work on it together.

His mother asked me to tea; I didn't see his father. She seemed nice enough. As we sat on the porch looking far out into the bay, she asked me about myself and my parents. When I told her my father taught at B.U., she said she'd heard it was "quite an up-and-coming university." I wanted to say, "Perhaps more up-and-coming than Harvard," but the lure of the darkroom controlled my tongue. I must have passed muster, for when I left she called out that I was to be sure and come back. I agreed only because Bob had already invited me.

July 8th–31st, 1965

I haven't had much time to write in my diary. Bob and I have been working nearly every day, except for the days when he's tired. Those days I wander the island and take pictures by myself. Thank goodness Mother's stopped worrying—she assumes I'm with Bob. I haven't told her that he's not always well. When I'm alone I can climb into places he wouldn't be able to go. This works out perfectly because I don't like to rub it in that he can't get to some spots. Sometimes, when we're together, he asks me to take pictures for him. That's okay, in fact it's great because he's mostly using color film, so I'm learning something about color shots, too. If it weren't for his difficulty climbing over rocks, I'd soon forget that he's had polio. To me he's a friend, a friend and a teacher with lots of patience in the darkroom—I'm not long on patience!

Much to my surprise, I no longer feel uncomfortable about the competition! Just the opposite, for he encourages me and teases me into doing things I want to do anyhow. I think he likes my crazy approach. I keep trying all kinds of things, from different settings to peeking the camera through holes in shrubs or rocks, lying down as near as I dare to waves splashing on boulders, pointing the camera to the sky, into a pool or anything that might give a wanted or different effect. You'll find some of the better results on the following pages—I won't bother to show you the worst!

There's no doubt, I have improved. You can see from one of my first sea pictures where the waves are running down hill and the horizon is tipped crazily, that I had a lot to learn. Bob's taught me how to check the horizon line in my viewfinder and, when it's impossible to keep the camera straight, how to correct the print in the darkroom. Obviously, to be a really first class photographer, you should do you own darkroom work—or, if you're lucky, find somebody like Bob to do it for you. We get along great. We're on the same wavelength, or maybe it's a complementary wavelength, for together we seem to make a whole. I don't suppose Bob feels as lucky as I do.

Wherever I see you mountains,
You show me a different face;
Sometimes you're far away, sometimes,
As near as my neighbor's place.

We've everything here from Storm to Clear,
From a man's content, to Joy or Fear,
From peaceful sun on a docile scene,
To sea rolling in—a windy whim;
The day or your lot reveals the plot.

August 2nd, 1965

August already! This last month has galloped along like a runaway horse. I haven't had to count the days, the hours, or even a passing minute—quite a miracle for me. I wish this summer would go on forever, but any illusions I had along those lines were taken care of by Mother and Father last night. On my way to bed, when I passed the stairwell, I heard them talking. Of course I stopped to eavesdrop—that's when you find out the truth.

"Do you think she should see the Stuart boy so much?" Mother was asking.

"Why not?" Father replied.

"Well, he's a cripple," Mother said.

The roots of my hair tingled and anger spewed up in my throat. I was about to run down and shout at her, when Father replied, "Bob's mind isn't crippled. You're more prejudiced than I thought. Anyhow, didn't you want her to have friends! I'd say Bob's about the best friend she's ever had, and the brightest, too."

"I was only thinking of what's best for her; a cripple could be a problem . . ."

"To be alive is a problem," Father interrupted, "but there you go again, jumping to conclusions. This is only a summer friendship, like a shipboard-romance—why, we may never come to this island again. It isn't our house

and I have to teach summer school next summer, besides Newton isn't Cambridge and by now you should know that B.U. is a long way from Harvard. I wish the friendship would go on, but, by the laws of probability—"

I, too, wished it would go on, but I wouldn't let myself think about that because I didn't see how it possibly could. Father wasn't quite right—some shipboard-romance!—but he was right about our return to the city, we'd no longer occupy the same space—Newton and 15 is a long way from Cambridge and 19! We'd be no longer bound by the sea.

August 4th, 1965

    After dinner, Bob picked me up in his car to take me to a nearby cove where I was to help him. It was a calm, clear evening, the best time and conditions for photographing reflections. When we were finished we sat in his car and talked. How I wished he'd put his arm around me, but it wasn't a shipboard-romance he'd been after! He did tell me of his hope to become a photographer for The Crimson; *after all* The Crimson *was almost as "prestigious" as the Harvard Football Team! Then he drove me home.*

August 7th, 1965

Mother complained that I'd been ignoring Shag—
"After all she's supposed to be your dog!" She's my dog,
okay, and sometimes she's my only friend, but I don't see
how I can take her to the Stuarts. The road's too danger-
ous, unless I walk all the way, and if I did there's still the
two red setters—they might not appreciate Shag and
she's so small, I worry that Bob'd trip over her. He'd be so
embarrassed. Yes, I've been missing her and she's missed
me, so I took her exploring this end of the island. We
found a beautiful grove of cedar. As the light caught the
tops of the trees, they danced in the rays of the sun.
My picture doesn't really tell the story, but it's the best I
could do. Sometimes my pictures seem so dead—at most
they catch a single moment of life. Trees are as alive as
we are, and dead trees are as dead as any dead human.
I've seen both. I remember my grandmother lying in an
open coffin. She was the wax-dummy of her original self.
I don't like that memory—her lying there so fake, so
unreal.

Shag and I went to the beach, too. She loves barking
at the spouting clams at low tide, and the scurrying
crabs, and when she was hot she waded into the sea and
sunk sighing into the cold water. Once thoroughly wet,
she rolled over, soaking her back, then dashed out and
tore up and down the beach, drying herself in her own
wind. I sat and watched until I couldn't stand it any
longer. I jumped up and tried to catch her. I finally fell
and we rolled over and over together, laughing. Do dogs
laugh? Of course they do.

I was surprised to find that the summer had brought changes to the beach. The wild grass had grown tall, crowned with great lengths of furry seeds, different from field grass—wild oats, I think. I wonder if you could make flour from the seeds. I chewed some and it tasted good. Maybe someday we'll have to eat these wild growing things if the people of the world continue in their crazy ways: pollution, over-population, or the atomic bomb. We've studied about these things in school. I wouldn't be surprised if over-population wasn't going to be the worst problem, and not just the under-developed countries. Right here, in the good old U.S.A., schools are over-crowded, and you have to line up for everything: parking, subways, in stores, buying tickets, even getting on and off roads. On the island you can forget all about that for a bit.

Maybe we'd be lucky if starvation came before the bomb, because at least there'd be something left. Here, on Outercliff, there are wild peas, sourgrass, rosehips, mushrooms, clams, crabs, mussels and of course, fish and lobsters—the beginning of a survival diet. I wonder if Shag isn't lucky not knowing about bombs and pollution. Sometimes I wish I didn't know.

August 10th, 1965

God, I feel awful. While I was munching oats, Bob fell off a high ledge on the back shore and broke his hip. He'd gone there to photograph rockpools—I knew he wanted to go, and I had planned to help him. If only I'd phoned him that day when I knew the tide was to be low in the afternoon. He could have phoned me, but he never would, he isn't one to ask for help. For hours he lay, unable to move, with that sound of the sea approaching, the tide inching its way nearer and nearer. It wasn't until early evening that his mother missed him. She called my mother to see if he was with me. I didn't have to take three whole days with Shag. Shag would have understood.

They flew him to Boston to the Children's Hospital. I would have thought he was too old for the Children's Hospital, but his mother told mine that once you had been treated for polio there, you always returned to their polio clinic.

August 11th, 1965

Bob's mother came back today. She phoned me this evening. That was really nice, to call so soon. I would have been pleased enough if she'd called tomorrow. Anyhow, she told me Bob was doing well. He was in some pain, but was as comfortable as could be expected. He was excited because they were going to try a new operation, removing part of the hip and replacing it with a shorter fake one in order to make his two legs more nearly even. It was an experimental operation but he was willing to be part of the experiment—if successful he'd be much better off.

She also said Bob wanted me to feel free to use his darkroom, but when I protested that I couldn't, she said that in return Bob wanted me to do him a favor—finish up some of his unfinished work. She had a list. That, I couldn't refuse, but I hoped it was things I knew how to do. She gave me Bob's address and asked me to write. I was glad she asked, for I wanted to write but after all, it was only a summer friendship!

August 14th, 1965

Dear Bob

I'm working on those things on your list. When your mother goes back to Boston in a few days, she'll bring the photos with her. I hope they're what you wanted.

Thanks for letting me use the darkroom. When Father heard about it he asked to see all my pictures; he hadn't seen hardly any since the first of the summer. He really liked them, so then he asked to read my diary. I asked why. He said perhaps he could get The University Press to do a small edition of it, but that the writing would have to pass muster, too. I said the diary was personal, so I'd have to think about it. He said wasn't the teacher going to read it. I said the teacher wasn't family! Well, the upshot was a compromise; he'd read the first part and then we'd talk, and he promised not to show it to Mother. He wants me to hurry up and finish the photographs. I miss your help!

Your mother told me about the operation. I keep whistling to the sky and trees to bring you luck. I gave an offering to the wind and waves, the way Indians used to give back the bones of a fish to the river that had been its home. I stood on the rocks, I held high your photo (one of two), the breeze was strong and off-shore, I chanted:

Bob will be well,
Bob will be well,
Oh, wind, who blows where it wills,
Oh, waves, who splash where they want,
Take my message "To whom it may concern";
Make Bob better, please, make Bob better.

and I let go. The white paper rose against the gray sky, dipping and whirling till I could no longer see it. It never crashed into the ocean, at least never as far as I could see—so, that's luck, I think!

Shag, whom you don't know well, sends you a lick, and I send you love and luck.

Best from Me,
Sandy

August 20th, 1965

Dear Bob

Thanks for your letter. Guess what! Father's decided to go ahead with the diary if they'll let him. He finally read the whole thing. He's going to help me with my spelling and point out the worst goofs, before he shows it to the University Press. I'm not sure whether I want them to print it or not—there's a lot about me I hadn't planned to make public!

Sorry about the pain. Hope now the operation is over you'll have less each day. Maybe there was a reason for the fall and my not being there to help (not that you expected me to be), maybe, just maybe, next summer you'll be a whole lot better. What you must have thought with the tide coming and no one to call to! Your mother says when the waves began to lap around your feet, you pulled yourself up on a rock. You're quite a hero around here!

Talking about being alone, everywhere I walk loneliness is in the air. One thinks of fall as a lonely season but perhaps one shouldn't, for despite the change, the going away, the leavetaking and even the dying (it can be part of next year's renewal), it is also a time for counting, for adding up and sometimes when you add it all up, the addition comes out on the plus side. Look at the asters, boldly thrusting their way out of the rocks, dangerously

near the reaching high tide—a little foolhardy, but they're blooming all over the place; I approve. And the apples; it was a good apple year no matter the shape or size of the tree: bent, straight, short or tall, even perfect, for I found a perfect apple tree and here is a picture of it with a mystery man in the background.

And so, my summer freedom is nearly over and I've only a few days left. I'd better get busy in the darkroom. Thanks for letting me use it. Wish you were here beside me for then I'd have more confidence. I don't really trust myself. I'm nervous, but I guess I'll learn to do it alone—we all have to in the end.

Take care of yourself. Do all of those boring exercises and maybe next summer you'll walk all over the island as you've never walked before.

Thinking of you
Sandy

The Apple Tree

Apples and an apple tree,
Patient in the autumn sun,
Waiting there for you or me,
To taste, or even just to come.

Whether we are there or not,
This apple tree remained
Anchored to this open spot
By miles of roots—a foothold gained,

Foothold in a soil so thin,
You'd be surprised it stands;
Stand it does, it grips within,
Where roots expand upon commands;

Commands ordered by terrain;
Soil that is deep with rocks,
Hard with clay, made soft by rain.
The apple doesn't mind hard knocks.

August 22nd, 1965
Dear Bob

Today I saw a lone heron. I moved up on him slowly, hoping he'd think I was a lumpy rock on the beach, but he didn't. As I snapped two pictures, too far away, I know, he lifted his great wings and rose, flapping them like a giant flag snapping slowly in a gentle breeze. I moved down nearer the water, but he never came back . . .

August 30th, 1965
Dear Bob

Saw ducks flocking for migration—or perhaps they were geese. Too far away for my inexperienced eyes to be able to tell. The summer people are flocking, too, and leaving. We're leaving September 2nd. I feel sad but at least I'll be seeing you soon. Father says when we get home he'll show me how to take the subway to the hospital. Will you help me with my pictures for the book? That

is if The University Press will print it for us. Father feels you could help us with the design and advise on which pictures to use and how to have them printed. I do too.
See you soon.

best
Sandy

Summer's End

The bay is empty of boats,
The beach curves to a lone rock.

Everywhere I walk there is a nothingness,
Except the gulls, splashing the cold low-tide mud,
As they hunt busily, those wily winners, their sweet shellfish dinners.

One lonely white lobster boat
Appears, and slips through the morning
Mist and haze. How lucky to have a place to go with a job to do.
We are lost without a daily destination,
And a daily return to another, a love or even a mother or a brother.

A chimney burned down its house,
To sit on a rock by itself.
Lost are the dreams which once were held by those whose hands held the stones;
Such dreams as you and I might have had. And so I cry a little,
As up high I see the geese flock, and down below I hear the waves crack and mock.

In a few days, I too, leave
This island of many moods.
It's time to go. I'm better I think for all I've seen and felt;
The swirling tides, the shifting shores, and the daily wounds,
But also the daily repair, in a place where birth and death are always in the air.

I've learnt a thing or two, here;
I hope to take with me something new,
Something other than the lessons I'd learn from a book.
Something of nature's ways and faith, who laughs lightly
At Man's tears, and makes its own plans for future years.

*
**
***

1000
copies of
this book, 200
hardcover and 800
softcover, have been
composed in Monotype Trump Mediaeval
and printed by offset on
Gleneagle paper.
The photographs have been reproduced
in halftone offset lithography. The design
is by the author and Bruce Kennett and the book
was produced at the Anthoensen Press
in Portland, Maine

****

****

****